THE BEST KEPT SECRET IN AMERICA

How to Retire at Any Age...
Even When The System Crashes

William A. Stanmeyer, J.D.

The Best Kept Secret In America
How to Retire at Any Age -- Even
When the System Crashes

By William A. Stanmeyer, J.D.

Printed in the United States of America

First Edition, January, 1996
Second Printing, May, 1996
Third Printing, June, 1996
Fourth Printing, July, 1996
Fifth Printing, August, 1996
Sixth Printing, September, 1996
Seventh Printing, October, 1996

ISBN: 0-9650992-0-2

Published by the Lincoln Communications Corporation
P.O. Box 15
Great Falls, VA 22066
(703) 749-3214

DEDICATION

This book is dedicated to my wife,

Judy,

whose patience has never failed;

And to all my friends who have the vision

to see what's coming -- and the courage to

take their future into their own hands.

CONTENTS

INTRODUCTION

"It was the best of times; it was
the worst of times."
-- Dickens, *A Tale of Two Cities*

****

A period of great change is "the best of times"-- for people who have the vision to profit by new economic arrangements... and "the worst of times" -- for those who continue to rely on old, crumbling institutions.

Whether a person's retirement will be "the best" or "the worst" of times depends on his vision... or whether one continues to rely on what's about to collapse.

A few years ago, some financial planners and I offered clients a computerized analysis of their long-term retirement preparations. The central question was:

"Will you have enough to retire?"

We analyzed the estimated rate of inflation, the future cost of college, likely portfolio growth, expected rate of return, and the amount of money deemed necessary in 10, 20, 30, or more years when retirement would begin.

For example, if in 20 years a person will need the purchasing power of $50,000 per year in *today's* dollars, the computer -- assuming 7% annual inflation -- would indicate need for $200,000 annual income in the year 2016.

At a 10% return on investment, the **capital fund** needed to generate such a sum will be $2,000,000. If the return is only 7%, the capital fund must approach $3,000,000. If investment return is a mere 5%, it will be $4,000,000.

Even the affluent usually fall far short of what they will need to retire in comfort.

Most people, facing daily living expenses and high college costs, put retirement saving "on the back burner."

When they finally turn their attention to this lurking challenge, most can do no more than form a small portfolio and "reposition assets" or "allocate resources" to increase yield--marginally.

Unfortunately, in today's changing economy, it is doubtful whether the average American even *has* enough investment assets to worry much about repositioning.

To base one's future security on marginal increments to a modest portfolio is to build on sand: it assumes there will be no serious setbacks, such as prolonged disability or loss of one's job.

But neither individual health nor national economic health is guaranteed.

As we begin the last four years of the 20th Century, an overwhelming number of Americans are not prepared to retire -- and *never will be*, unless they take a radically different approach to preparation.

The first part of this book explores the challenge of paying for retirement from traditional sources: job... social security... pensions... personal savings. It also analyzes how the electronic revolution impacts conventional employment and retirement plans.

The second part outlines a time-leveraged method to create sufficient income in one's older years. This system can generate as much cash flow in three to five years as do traditional investments which took 20-30 years to put together.

The first part, like a doctor's diagnosis of a very sick patient, is grim. The second part, like a prescription for an amazingly effective medicine and highly successful therapy, should give the reader grounds for hope and optimism.

Retirement will be the best of times for people who use time-leveraging; it will be the worst of times for those who lack the vision to change but insist on clinging to the crumbling old ways.

CHAPTER 1: BABY-BOOMERS AND "THE RULE OF 72"

"The future ain't what it used to be."
-- Yogi Berra

****

Flaws in the Conventional Wisdom

The traditional approach to retirement recommends a mix of three sources of income: Social Security, company pension plans, and personal savings.

For this approach to work, there has to be a solvent Social Security system, widespread and well-funded corporate pension plans, and a high rate of personal savings.

Further, we must know what "retirement expenses" will be. And they must not be too high.

Unfortunately, there is grave doubt whether the traditional mix will work; but considerable certainty that expenses will be far more than most people think.

Mugged by the "Rule of 72"

Albert Einstein said that the way compound interest works is a mathematical mystery which even he did not fully understand. But it does work; and there is a simple formula to figure real-world results.

To find out how many years it will take for compound interest to double your money, divide the interest rate you are earning into the number 72.

Thus if the interest rate is 4%, it will take 18 years for $1,000 to double to $2,000. But at 7%, it will take only 10 years. If the rate is

10%, you will double your money in 7.2 years. Needless to say, a 12% interest rate will double your money in only 6 years.

The Rule applies to negative compounding, too: if you want to know how long it will take for all prices to double, just crank your anticipated inflation rate into the same equation.

The math is the same. At a 4% inflation rate, in 18 years a $15,000 auto will cost $30,000. If the inflation rate averages 7% over the decade, a $150,000 house in 1990 will be $300,000 at the turn of the century.

Indeed, over the last 30 years, the annual inflation rate has been almost 7% per year. At times it spiked up sharply, as in 1980-81, when it was over 12%. And sometimes it dropped down, as in 1994-95, when, if we can believe the Government, inflation was less than 3%.

To plan prudently, a person should assume that every ten years prices will double.

Reality Check

The way to start planning is to *pretend you quit work tomorrow*. How much income will you need tomorrow -- and each year for the rest of your life?

Many financial planners counsel 70% to 80% of current income. But this could be too low. One needs to factor in medical expenses and long-term "assisted living" care.

Next ask: "What assets do I now own, which will generate that income?" The sum of such assets is my *capital fund*.

The third question: "Assume an X% return on investment; how big a capital fund will I need to generate, say, $30,000?... or $60,000... or $150,000?" Answer: at a 7% return, tomorrow you will need $430,000 to generate a mere $30,000... or over $2,000,000 to provide an annual $150,000.

But if a person is 40 years old and expects to retire at 60, the Rule of 72 will mug him! When prices double in 10 years, and then *double once again* in the second ten years,

> **merely to maintain $30,000-per-year in today's purchasing power, he will need $860,000 in the bank a decade from now, and $1,720,000 in 20 years.**

Of course, a person satisfied with $30,000 is not one who can save and invest his way to $860,000 in only ten years. Indeed, by saving **all** of his gross income -- an impossible task -- he still falls short by hundreds of thousands of dollars.

What about a professional -- call him "Dr. Jones," -- who wants to maintain a $150,000 per year standard of living? If *tomorrow* he needs $2,000,000 in the bank, then in ten years he will need $4,000,000, in 20 years $8,000,000.

What are the chances that he can put enough money into investments over the next two decades to grow to $8,000,000 by the year 2016?

If your crystal ball shows that prices will take longer to double, then use another example, with more conservative assumptions. Grant that a friend, "Marie Smith," age 45, could retire on $40,000 per year tomorrow. Assume inflation will be 5% annually for the next 45 years.

Marie Smith will then fit into the following pattern:

Age	Income Needed
59	$ 80,000
73	160,000
88	320,000

But if we peer into a murky crystal ball and see only gradual... minor... linear... price increases over 40 or more years, we're probably fooling ourselves.

"Those who will not learn history," said Santyana, "are doomed to live it over."

Past economic history has been stormy. The Crash of 1929 ushered in temporary deflation. But repeated episodic explosions of inflation have pushed prices up like a rocket. In 1980-81, prices increased over 12% per year.

If we "live over" past history, the future will probably bring further explosive periods of change. Most Americans, whether "Dr. Jones" or "Marie Smith," have not faced up to the cost of the journey into the future.

Stark Statistics

The lead article of my Accountant's autumn, 1994, Newsletter "*Will You Have Any Money At Retirement?*" pointed out that 98% of Americans will have little or none. Here are the numbers:

Out of every 100 people reaching age 65

> 1 will be wealthy
> 9 will have income between $15,000 and $24,999
> 33 will be dead
> 57 will be **dead broke.**

In other words, following the conventional system which tells us, "Go to school, work hard, get good grades, and go out and get a good job," as many as **90 out of 100 will have nothing to show for their 40 years of work**.

And if you agree that an income between $15,000 and $24,999 is nothing to fax home about, then **99 out of 100 have almost nothing financial to show for the passage of 40 years.**

They say that to get the attention of a mule, one must hit it across the nose with a two-by-four. Some people are as stubborn as a mule. If someone you know won't pay attention, swing this fact at his nose:

The Social Security Administration has calculated that of the people currently receiving benefits,

> 45% depend on relatives
> 30% depend on charity
> 23% are still working
> 2% are self-sustaining.

Naturally, professionals like us doctors, dentists, attorneys and others think *we* will be in the 2%. But a few lawyer friends have told me, with feigned nonchalance, "I don't have enough to retire on, so I'll just work till I drop." I used to think that was the answer. But it is not.

If a man "drops" into his grave, he has not created a long-term problem for his wife and children. *But if he drops into disability --* stroke, Alzheimers, heart attack -- as is more likely for men 60 to 70 years old, how will he crank out all those "billable hours" his firm insists on?

It would be prudent for professionals to ask whether the last twenty years of their lives will be as energetic as the middle forty.

It's hard to make money when your eyes are dim and your hand is shaking.

"The Coming Retirement Crunch"

In its June 13, 1994 issue, *U.S. News & World Report* warned ("Baby Boomers, Wake Up") that most people's retirement ships have holes in the hull. Most seriously underestimate the amount of money they will need. The bottom line:

> **For each $10,000 of income per year in today's dollars that a person now 48 will need between age 65 and age 90, he must have $330,000 in a tax-deferred savings program when his retirement begins.**

So someone age 48 today who wants the equivalent of $50,000 per year in purchasing power starting at 65 and continuing till age 90 will need $1,700,000. So says T. Rowe Price Associates, using an inflation rate of 4% and a 7% return-on-investment.

A year later, undeterred that this prophecy evoked a massive yawn, *U.S. News* (June 12, 1995) again swung the two-by-four at the nose of the mule.

They presented a package of statistics even more dismal than in 1994; in sum:

> **A 40-year-old who wants $10,000 of annual income in 1995 dollars between age 65 and 90 will need $469,000 in a tax-deferred retirement account at age 65.**

As everyone knows, $10,000 per year is not much. Most people will need at least $40,000. A person 40 in 1996 who wants the purchasing power of that $40,000 per year -- in 1996 dollars -- beginning 25 years later when he or she reaches age 65, must have squirreled away $1,900,000.

Getting hit by the difference between where one is financially and where one ought to be is called "the retirement crunch."

"Crunch!" A person thinks of two 300-pound defensive linemen sacking one 200-pound quarterback.

5

In 1994, *U.S. News* recommended that people put their money aggressively into stocks. A year later, doubtless to avert panic among us financial arm-chair quarterbacks, the magazine proposed a new way to dodge the charging linemen.

The editors told us aging financial quarterbacks to keep scrambling: **just keep working.** They found a few happy 70-year-old consultants, travel agents, jobholders and business people. These septuagenarians have it made, the magazine explained, because they just keep making it.

Don't you feel relieved? Are you saying to yourself, "Why didn't I think of that?"

Or are you mumbling: "Hey, wait a minute! These people are a *tiny* minority: they are healthy, have a marketable skill, and made good money in their earlier years.

"What about people who are not healthy, who have no marketable skill, who never made 'good money'"? What if there aren't any "good jobs" left for 70-year-olds after the 30- and 40-year-olds have picked them over?

I believe there are more white-haired widows wiping tables at McDonalds than grandmothers leading tours to Sweden.

Anyway, lest you think that *U.S. News* is a lone alarmist, glance at the series published by *USA TODAY* (May 8-11, 1995), which sprinkled the pages with article headings such as these:

- **Poll: Only 44% Are Preparing for Retirement**
- **Pensions: Not as Safe as You Think**
- **No Savings Means: More Work Longer**
- **Street Talk: Boomers Still Trail In Savings Game**

Perhaps these abstract warnings will have more impact if we look at a simple topic: how to pay for what you *eat*. Farris Baker Watts, a fine Washington, D.C. metro-area investment advisory firm, provides this page on the costs of food. Remember, as you glance down this chart, that a $15.00 *daily* food allowance does not permit many forays to the local French restaurant... or even to Shoneys.

Bringing Home the Bacon: What It Will Cost You to Eat During Retirement

Year	Daily Food Cost	Yearly Food Cost
1	$15.00	$5,475.00
2	15.60	5,694.00
3	16.22	5,920.00
4	16.87	6,157.55
5	17.54	6,402.10
6	18.24	6,657.60
7	18.97	6,924.05
8	19.73	7,201.45
9	20.52	7,489.80
10	21.34	7,789.10
11	22.19	8,099.35
12	23.08	8,424.20
13	24.00	8,760.00
14	24.96	9,110.40
15	25.96	9,475.40
16	27.00	9,855.00
17	28.08	10,249.20
18	29.20	10,658.00
19	30.37	11,085.05
20	31.58	11,526.70
		$162,954.30

"This example assumes you eat 3 meals a day over a 365 day year and food prices increase at a constant rate of 4% per year."

Is that realistic?

Not Enough Eggs In the Nest Egg Basket

Numerous studies come to the same grim conclusion: unless we do something radically different, 80 to 90% of us will face financial difficulty or disaster in our later years.

Next time you are at a meeting -- PTA, Kiwanis, alumni, or your church -- look around at the others present. Of 50 people there, 40 to 45 of them will have a terrible retirement.

Of course, some other fellow may be doing the same mental calculation. He sees the same 50. Does he count *you* as one of the 40 or one of the 10? On what grounds do you argue that he's wrong, if he puts you among the 40...?

A study conducted by Arthur D. Little for Oppenheimer Management estimated that nearly 80% of households will have **less than half the annual income they will need** to retire in comfort. Says Jon S. Fossel, Oppenheimer's chairman:

> **"Few Americans today lived through the Great Depression, but at this rate, that's exactly what most people's retirements will be like.... [M]any will find themselves struggling to simply make ends meet."**

If you say, "That may be a problem for other people, but *I* am a professional and *I* know how to plan ahead," The Merrill Lynch Baby Boom Retirement Index might give you pause: it reports that it is the *higher* earners -- many of them professionals -- who will have a harder time meeting their retirement needs than the lower earners!

The Vanishing Pension Plan

Merrill Lynch estimated that married couples between the ages of 35 and 45, who earn $20,000 to $40,000 total per year and have pension benefits, can expect to have 49.03% of the retirement income they will need to feel comfortable.

Forget the decimals. It simply means: "about half" what they need.

But other couples in the same age range, also having pensions, who earn over $100,000 per year, will have 47.87% of the income they will need to live to *their* standards.

The winner, by a whisker, is the poorer group! They come two percent closer to having *only one-half what they will need* than does the rich group!

So both the affluent and the working poor are in the same boat. A very leaky one.

How can this be? For one thing, only about one-third of Americans have a pension plan at work. Second, *many pension plans are grossly underfunded* and could shortchange them.

8

Between 1970 and 1990, most large organizations invested their pension funds *conservatively*. For those twenty years, they became accustomed to much higher interest rates than today.

But since 1992, interest rates have plunged. Suddenly pension plans that had used high rates in their assumptions faced being unable to meet future payouts.

So they jumped into the stock market. By fall of 1995, many had become seriously overexposed in stocks: some have 50% - 70% of their assets invested in this volatile market.

If the market hits a "correction"... i.e., collapse... i.e., *crash*... the fund managers will have to tell their employees that pension benefits will be cut 25% - 30%... or more.

Moreover, many corporate pension plans are top-heavy with the companies' own stock. A person may have worked for a great company, like Mobil, Ford, or IBM, but if its stock drops sharply, income from his or her pension will drop as well.

> If you've been a teacher or a middle-management executive for almost 40 years and are about to retire, but the school system or company informs you that -- because of fund underperformance--your pension benefits unfortunately will have to be cut by more than 30%... where does that leave you?

The Government will bail you out, right? Not if its own bucket is full of holes. In that case, you will keep sinking.

Recently the Government's own Pension Benefit Guaranty Corporation released a worrisome report which declared pension underfunding has increased *for the fifth year in a row*. They admitted that "...current law is not working...."

The *Wall Street Journal* has reported that "total benefit obligations of the 50 most underfunded private pension plans exceeded their assets by *$38.05 billion* at the end of 1992, an increase of nearly $9 billion from a year earlier.... Underfunded plans can be a threat to retirees' future pension[s]...."

The Pioneer Spirit

In the pre-Civil War decades, and again in the period after it, Americans pressed westward to find a better life. They sought a place to settle.

As they planned their journey across Badlands, through uncharted forests, and along the edge of deserts, the pioneers of that era had to estimate the provisions they needed to carry.

It makes no sense to trudge a thousand miles only to die of thirst with the destination almost in sight.

Today every American makes a "journey" not over land, but through time. Yet few Americans have calculated the increased cost of the last twenty years of the trip.

It makes no sense to work forty years only to run out of money with the goal of retirement in sight.

We have to plan for two challenges: first, prices will probably double and redouble in twenty years; so we need to make our income double twice over that time. Second, just when we need more income, our own health and strength will be declining.

It will be *harder* to make money at the very time when we will need making money to be easier.

The conventional response is: get a higher paying job... hang on to it longer... and save more of your income from it.

Crunch! That play will lose yardage. It runs head-on into the new economic revolution....

That revolution is demolishing the conventional ways of earning a living, but, fortunately, creating new ways to solve the problem, which the second half of this essay will explain.

CHAPTER 2: THE NEW ECONOMIC REVOLUTION

> "Holmes! Holmes! The hounds -- the
> hounds did not bark." Holmes paused,
> puffing inscrutably on his pipe. After a few
> moments he smiled, a glint in his eye.
> "Precisely, my dear Watson. The hounds
> did <u>not</u> bark. And that is the clue."
> -- Arthur Conan Doyle, *The Adventure of
> Silver Blaze*, paraphrased and embellished.

****

The clue: the murderer had not aroused dogs bred to guard estates. The dogs knew him. So he must have been a close friend, a servant, a relative, or other frequent visitor.

Holmes used something *absent* -- the mastiffs barking -- to identify something present, a quality -- familiarity with the intruder -- that made it possible to solve the mystery.

To unravel the mystery of retirement economics we need only look at what increasingly is *not* there, but granted our expectations, we still think should be: *the Job.*

According to *Business Week* (May 9, 1994), there were over 3,000 corporate jobs cut *each day* during the first quarter of 1994. Here are layoff highlights, from early 1991 to spring 1994:

Corporation	Jobs Cut
IBM	86,000
AT&T	83,600
General Motors	74,000
Sears	50,000
Boeing	30,000
NYNEX	22,000
Hughes Aircraft	21,000
Proctor & Gamble	18,000
GTE	17,000
Martin-Marietta	15,000
DuPont	14,800
Eastman Kodak	14,000
Phillip Morris	14,000
PharMor	13,000
Bank of America	12,000
Aetna	11,800
GE Aircraft Engines	10,250
McDonnell Douglas	10,200
Bell South	10,200

Downsizing continues. In November of 1995, newspapers reported that in the prior month there were 41,335 layoffs nationwide. In December 1995, the *Washington Post* reported 55,000 more layoffs occurred that month. Indeed, shortly before this essay went to press, AT&T alone announced planned dismissals of yet another 40,000 employees in coming months.

The Job is no longer there -- and that is the clue!

Lying on the Track in Front of the Engine of Progress

Every major economic change in recent centuries has dislocated what is now called "the job market." Economic change always upsets people who rely on past patterns to deal with the future.

- Steam and gas engines changed transportation patterns: trains and trucks replaced most domestic barge shipping and all horse-drawn transport and wiped out thousands of jobs in those industries.

- Companies which manufactured carbon paper all but disappeared once Xerox perfected the photocopier.

- The switch to electronic fuel injectors from mechanical carburetors was good for all drivers... but carburetor manufacturers and mechanics lost their jobs.

- Audiocassettes replaced vinyl records, and only twenty years later, CDs are replacing cassettes.

In each case, manufacturing jobs using the older technology evaporated.

But in the 1990s, there is a difference: in the past the introduction of new products and new technologies eradicated obsolescent jobs. But in their place it created new ones.

In earlier times a person could keep on saving for retirement: the buggy whip factory disappeared but automobile factories took its place -- and buggy-whip workers got jobs at Ford and kept right on earning and saving.

Today jobs are not just being replaced; they are disappearing. The hounds are not barking. The jobs are not there.

And that is the clue... to what a person needs to do: find a way to generate income -- now and in retirement -- *without a job.*

Downward Mobility, "Dumpies," and The End of the Job
- *Cover story, Business Week (March 22, 1992), "Downward Mobility."* Recounts the plight of Allen S., who at age 48 was laid off by Cigna, lost his $50,000 annual income, his savings, his wife, and all his retirement assets.

If misery loves company, Allen might relate to the later story of Gerald F., M.B.A., who in 1991 lost his $57,000 administration job with a downsizing office equipment retailer. By spring of 1992, he was on $270-per week unemployment and had just received notice of foreclosure on the house his family had occupied for 26 years.

- *Cover story, U.S. News & World Report, (June 28, 1993), "Where Did My Career Go?"...inside title, "White Collar Wasteland."* Recounts middle management's financial skid. David S., a 30-year-old accountant with IBM, became "surplus," lost his $40,000 job, and landed on his feet -- sort of -- as a bookkeeper at a real estate firm -- at $21,000.

13

Also notes Jim R., 56, former IBM financial analyst, now earning $10 per hour collecting tolls at a bridge over the Hudson; and 35-year-old Jim T., who lost his $60,000 computer sales job, had to declare bankruptcy, and now scrambles to make an interior decorating business work.

These men are members of the new class of "Dumpies": they've been dumped.

"The Contingent Work Force"
- *Cover story, Fortune (September 19, 1994), "The End of the JOB,"* with a subhead calling the Job a "social artifact" that is going the way of the dinosaur.

Cover picture: sleeveless factory worker straining with two-foot wrench to turn lug nut on huge iron fly wheel. Must be file photo from the 1920s.

The message, in almost syllogistic steps, goes like this:

The Job is an artificial 19th century construct. It is too rigid for elastic problems.... Jobs discourage accountability and are not socially adaptive.... The trend is to the **contingent work force** -- temps, part-timers, consultants, contract workers.... Companies do not need a rigid 13-tier hierarchy; 5 will do, or what is called the "project cluster." So middle management will wither away.

What about saving for retirement as this goes on? We can be sure that the gentlemen mentioned above -- and thousands of others in middle management -- have not saved much since 1992 -- unless they found a new way of making money.

Former manager types spend most of their efforts treading water just trying to stay afloat. Retirement saving will be later. If at all.

Handwriting on the Wall
According to the Old Testament Book of Daniel, during a debauched banquet, wicked King Belshazzar watched a mysterious hand write on the palace wall words no one could interpret. So he called the prophet Daniel, who translated:

"Your kingdom is ended.... You have been found wanting.... Your kingdom is given to the Medes and Persians."

Later that night, Darius the Mede invaded the palace, killed Belshazzar, and conquered Babylon.

Today, there is "handwriting on the wall" in press releases from corporate America extolling "streamlining" and "strategic restructuring" and "outsourcing" for "higher efficiency." Translated, it says:

The computer will eventually perform any human service that one can program a computer to do.

This development delivers a one-two punch. First, in many jobs a computer simply replaces the job holder.

Second, a computer user, with phone and fax, can create intense new competition for those people who still do have jobs. It's happening in many fields.

1. Banking
Automatic Teller Machines now handle many bank services that human tellers once provided. Business analysts predict that in eight to ten years half the nation's bank teller jobs will disappear -- and most of those remaining will be part-time.

- First Union Corporation moved most teller and customer service employees to part time. Its goal is to increase part-timers from 40% to 75% by 1996.

- First National of Chicago proposed a $3.00 service charge each time a customer uses a human teller in transactions which a machine -- i.e., computer -- can handle, such as deposits, withdrawals, and balance inquiries.

- A senior VP at another big bank admitted one reason for the rush to automation is to avoid paying fringe benefits. He is excited about cutting health-care expenses at his bank.

- In October 1995, I received a mail solicitation from Citibank; it asked me to try "Direct Access Banking":

"Imagine being able to pay [your electric company] from the computer in your den. Or to send a check to your aunt in Florida from an advanced new screen telephone in your living room. Now you can check your balances, transfer funds, open and link accounts... 24 hours a day, seven days a week."

They could have added: *"And you won't be creating a job for a human bank clerk."*

All in all, experts expect that the nation's 441,000 bank tellers will drop to as few as 250,000. For these people "the handwriting is on the wall"; it shouldn't take Daniel to interpret it.

2. Real Estate: the End of the Agent?

The year 2000 may be deemed "The End of the Age." By then we may have seen the end of the Agent.

- A company in Minnesota videotapes neighborhoods in major cities. The scenes will be on computer. Soon you will be able to "house hunt" from the privacy of a realtor's office.

- Computerized multiple listing consolidation in regional areas will, by mid-1997, link 30,000 agents and provide instant access to data comparing house values, tax assessments, and even school test scores. The system will display color photos of house exteriors and, for a fee, a dozen inside photos.

Detailed maps will show a house's proximity to schools, churches, parks, shopping centers, and subway stops, and anything special about the house.

No longer will house hunters spend a day driving to six or eight scattered homes to locate the farmhouse-looking colonial with a fully covered front porch that they want.

Soon an entire real estate deal, even settlement and utilities cutoff, will be done electronically. By mid-1997, your computer will access lists, rates, and services of mortgage lenders, title insurance companies, and settlement attorneys.

Buyers will get qualified mortgage approvals through the system even before house hunting. After the seller signs a contract, the computer will track the settlement process so all parties know what tasks remain, such as termite inspection.

At its inception, the local system will permit access only to real estate agents and brokers. Ordinary buyers and sellers will be kept out.

But does anyone believe that whatever <u>can</u> be done by computers will not be done? An increasingly

16

computer-literate populace will find a way to do it themselves -- and cut out the "middleman."

Why pay a seller's broker 6% of your $300,000 sale price, they will ask, to click his computer "mouse" across a screen at his office when *you* can click *your* "mouse" across your screen in your own den at home -- and save $18,000?

Looking for a new house? Why engage a "buyer's broker" to gather data for you at his office when you can do it from your home computer?

There goes that "buyer's broker" commission, $9,000 on a $300,000 purchase.

Will all this happen overnight? No. Will it happen everywhere? Probably not right away. Will it happen? Almost certainly Yes. Will it happen sooner or later?

Sooner. The pace of change is accelerating. When the Ice Age came, it too may have come quickly. Explorers have found ice-frozen mastodons, still chewing grass. Too bad they did not know how to adapt.

3. Online Stock Trading without a Stock Broker

The rush is on to roll out computerized brokerage services. In October of 1995, National Discount Brokers launched trading over the Internet.

AccuTrade, Inc., which began its PC trading service in 1993, has enhanced it with a wireless option. Customers can copy portfolio information, carry it around in a hand-held device, and trade orders or update information through a wireless modem.

They use voice-recognition technology with call-back features: AccuTrade's computer calls customers back after they place orders to confirm the trade.

These and other companies are ushering in an era when investors can circumvent human beings altogether.

The result? Gradually a growing segment of investors will come to believe they do not need to deal with a Broker to get advice, or call one to make a trade. As with ATM banking machines, so also in the securities marketing industry: the "middleman" grows superfluous.

AccuTrade can run a national operation solely from its Omaha base. And National Discount's mere five offices have an international reach. Unlike Merrill Lynch, Smith Barney, Wheat First, and all the other high-quality and high-visibility traditional stock advisory firms, these upstart newcomers have minimal brick-and-mortar investment.

One may be sure that Merrill Lynch *et al* will find a way to "downsize" and reach out to the PC-literate investors who like technology and see no reason for a full-service Broker.

But, like the little computer firms that began pecking away at IBM's market dominance back twenty years ago, Accutrade and National Discount and their imitators will surely cut into the profits of -- and need for -- full-time Brokers with the traditional stock trading firms.

So the competition for accounts, especially among the younger Brokers striving to build a loyal clientele who will provide them repeat business, will intensify.

In a "survival-of-the-fittest" battle, some will not survive.

4. Hyper-Competition among Professionals

Soon the international suppliers of *products* which invade America will be joined by international suppliers of *services*.

Initially it was Japanese cars and TV sets. Then came clothes, toys, briefcases, calculators, etc. from Korea, Taiwan, and Hong Kong.

Directly or indirectly these "peaceful invaders" replaced American jobs. Now we are moving into a time when the *professions* will face much the same competition.

Saturation in a field can occur in different ways. One is to produce far more practitioners than the market can absorb; for example, the annual graduation of 33,000 new lawyers has all but saturated the legal profession.

A second way a business loses market share occurs when someone offers a better supply of a similar service: when communications megapolies like Time-Warner begin to offer television "movies-on-demand" through telephone lines or by satellite, Blockbuster may be busted.

A third way a field can become saturated is by *introducing competent foreign competitors who will work for a far lower wage.*

The trend is obvious at 7-11s, where the clerks are more often Vietnamese, Hispanic, or Afghanistani -- not Anglo-American... at many dry cleaners, where the clerks are often Korean or Chinese... at McDonalds, where many burger-providers are Hispanic, Indian, or other immigrant stock.

In their struggle with language and acculturation, these first-generation Americans seem little threat to the jobs of high-paid professionals, and to the retirement money these jobs produce.

But their better educated countrymen *are* such a threat. Consider this insight, paraphrased from TAIPAN, a futurist investment advisory:

> **The people hiring don't need Americans. This is not about people with green cards but about a person in another country who can do your job -- from his home in India, or Thailand, or wherever -- as well as you can... and certainly *cheaper*.**

> **Why pay a costly American architect to draft plans for your home... when for 1/3 the price a Bangladeshi architect will use his computer to create a model of your proposed house and FAX it to you for approval?**

It is likely that global competition will put many white-collar Americans into the unemployment line. With a computer and a phone, you can perform many "white-collar" tasks from anywhere in the world.

> **Thanks to data transmission technologies, a person can now hire architects, engineers, lawyers, and other professionals from anywhere on earth.**

More "handwriting on the wall."

Eventually Americans will have to compete on a nearly equal basis with everyone else in the world.

> **If an international company needs a middle-level executive, will it hire a German who can speak English fluently, or an American who can't speak German at all...? Russian scientists and engineers are willing to work for $200 a month; so who will hire the American at $200 per day?**

In a recent book, *The Capitalist Manifesto*, James Dale Davidson argued the same thesis:

Even skilled workers will face intense competition.

Ever greater numbers of Information Age workers will be exposed to price competition from overseas workers. Twenty years ago, Davidson says, if you wished to hire a computer programmer or a Wall Street analyst, you were obliged to hire him in a large American city. But

> **"Today you can hire 27 stock analysts in India for the price of one Wall Street analyst. Instant communication makes any part of the world only a moment away by fax, phone or modem."**

Besides futurists, newspaper writers occasionally see the problem as well. For example, in a *Washington Post* article titled "Unwelcome Guests," (August 14, 1995, A17), Lars-Erik Nelson reports the plight of a certain Larry Richards, a contract software programmer who wanted to figure out why his hourly freelance rate had dropped from $45 to $30.

By posing as a businessman, Richards quickly obtained Labor Department permission to import twenty computer programmers from India with a proposed pay rate of $5.00 per hour.

The same column told of an insurance company in New Jersey that laid off 250 workers and then replaced them with "temps" from India. Either way, whether the architect comes electronically or the "temp" comes physically, ambitious skilled foreigners are ready, willing, and able to challenge you and me for a share of the employment pie.

Not all are from India. Koreans, Chinese, Malaysians, Indonesians, and Vietnamese are as willing as the Poles, Russians, and East Germans to work in the new electronic world for less than half what Americans used to command.

As Davidson counsels:

> **"Don't assume you can do the same thing for the same employer for thirty years; those days are gone. Even if your job is the highest of high tech, new technology can render it obsolete very quickly.... The future is going to be very hard on people who merely rent their time to a boss."**

Market forces -- international market forces -- dropped Larry Richards' income from $45 to $30 per hour, a 33% decline. He had to compete with high-quality, able technicians from another country. People willing to work for a relative pittance.

With income cut 33%, his ability to save dropped 33% -- or more: just to stay even, current cash flow usually goes to immediate needs. Pay the mortgage, repair the car, put braces on his child's teeth. Save later. Maybe.

Nor will professionals who work with their hands escape. The master auto mechanic and the experienced dentist face new forms of competition: the universal urge toward "discount shopping" has spawned group-buying clubs for every service from auto tune-ups to root canals. Join one of these associations, get their "Provider Directory," and if you are willing to drive an extra 20 miles, you can well save $100 - $200 on car or teeth maintenance.

When computerized lists of discount providers become widespread, the downward pressure on professionals' fees will intensify.

How can a dentist whose office overhead is 50% to 75% of his gross income find extra money to save for retirement when he must reduce his fees just to attract a continuing flow of patients?

5. Downsizing the City

This one is subtle. Our cities are turning into dinosaurs. The super-metropolis -- New York, Chicago, Los Angeles, and dozens of others -- is an idea whose time has come... and gone.

Have you noticed that when a magazine lists "The 10 best places to live in" in America, they never mention our really big cities?

Live in Aspen, but not Denver. Settle in Rockford, but not Chicago. Locate in Charlottesville, but for heaven's sake, not in Washington, D.C. Get the idea?

People are leaving -- or want to leave -- the big cities for many reasons: crime... air pollution... congestion... sometimes contaminated water... no parking... poor schools... high taxes... collapsing "infrastructure" (How many hours do people waste daily in New York detouring around a street closed by a broken water main?)

The cities symbolize and physically express the spirit,   attitude, morals, priorities, morale, and common notions of how to live and how to make a living... of an epoch... and of a people who are changing.

Answer this question honestly: if you could work in your own neighborhood, would you jump in your car at o'dark thirty every morning to drive 25 miles in an hour... pay $8.00 daily parking... cram yourself into an office cubicle 30 stories up?   And probably not even have a window...?

Only to repeat the process in reverse at 5 or 6 or 7 at night... every day... five days a week... 50 weeks a year... for 40 years...?

If we waste two hours a day commuting... for 40 years, we have spent 500 hours a year or 20,000 hours of our lives.   Sitting in the car. Listening to the traffic report.

> "There's an overturned 18-wheeler on I-95. All traffic
> northbound is stopped. With the snow, it'll be some time
> before wrecking equipment can open the road...."

Over 20,000 hours dribbled away: 2,000 work days of 10 hours each. *That's five years!*

Residents of Aspen, Rockford, and Charlottesville have no such problem. They get home in time to watch their kids' soccer games.

Skyscrapers are large filing cabinets where people who file paper are filed. Many of them are lacking even the tenants that the owners need to make their mortgage payments.

In mid-October 1995, downtown office space vacancy in Dallas was 37%, in Miami, 27%, in Baltimore, 25%. In Detroit there are so many empty skyscrapers that people joke mordantly about 400-foot headstones in a graveyard of a past era.

"Fortune 500" company layoffs have made about 250 million square feet of office space available for sublease, the equivalent of 250 Chrysler Buildings.

If they had the choice, most people would rather work at home. Forget that overturned 18-wheeler. Watch their daughter's soccer game. Take a coffee break anytime, because no boss is watching. Have "casual day" every day, not just Friday.

The trend to working at home is accelerating. In 1980 fewer than 1,000,000 people worked out of their homes. Today there are almost 40,000,000.

Sure, many of them are those middle management types who got laid off by IBM, DuPont, Sears, AT&T, and dozens of other companies in the rush to "downsize." Some sit at their computer sending out resumes in search of the next job; some are Consultants looking for the next retainer.

But many are people still "with" corporate employers but doing their thing from home. Some are like the high-powered business consultant *Forbes* described, who wagered with his friends that he could work for his clients from anywhere, and *they would not know where he was.*

He set up a remote-control voice mail in New York and then positioned his phone and fax and computer next to his pool at a villa in the Virgin Islands.

He made his usual pile of money. But for six months nobody knew where he was. They thought he was in New York, detouring around a water main break. But he was in St. Thomas, rubbing suntan lotion on his shoulders. Typing on a laptop.

6. Virtual Meetings

And he does not use -- yet -- the **"Being There Wall."** Soon it will be possible for two or more people to have a "conference" by two-way television, while each remains at his office -- *or even in his own home.* Sony is working on a video system that is only a few inches deep but has a 20-square-foot picture screen.

No more speaker phones. No more conference calls. Turn on the "wall" and speak with anybody, face-to-face. Anywhere in the world. The "wall" is *portable.*

With such a device, a person could do business at any time... without rush hour stress... wasted commute time... or fear for personal security at night.

If men and women in business can meet with colleagues from Denver or attend a sales seminar in New York, *without leaving their office in Dallas or their home in Chicago*, many will reduce or eliminate airline and hotel use.

Drive to airport... stand in line... pay hundreds for ticket... wait... ride plane many hours... wait for

23

luggage... cab to hotel... pay additional hundreds for hotel and meals... repeat process to return... miss a week with spouse and kids.

These stressful activities *do not enhance the value of the meeting itself.* A two-day business conference with nationwide attendance absorbs three or four days of time.

But in their intense search for efficiency, many cost-conscious companies will turn to the "Being There Wall" to save time and money.

Is this fanciful? -- just science fiction? -- a futurist's day dream? Look to today's newspaper, business section:

> **"Lockheed Martin, AT&T Plan Satellite Services. Video Conferencing, Other Applications Seen.** A new space race is on, as companies jockey... to offer high-capacity Internet access and video conferencing directly from satellites to homes and businesses... using two-foot diameter satellite dishes."

Lockheed Martin's "Astrolink" will use nine satellites to deliver voice, video and data at speeds 600 times faster than today's modems. It will carry business, medical, educational, and industrial information.

AT&T plans a video-telephone network in the sky: to offer wireless phones, electronic messaging, financial transactions... and *video conferencing.*

Traditional office buildings, where so many people are filed, are about to feel an electronic earthquake.

Downtowns of big cities as places of work, and not just quaint relics of a bygone era to visit, like a tavern decorated in an 1890s motif, are an embodied idea whose time has passed.

Once again, the reason is computer, satellite, fax, and phone.

The cities will downsize. Commercial rentals values will drop. Department stores and downtown shopping malls will decline. The tax base will erode. The featherbed for city workers is over.

It will become harder for cities to fund their workers' pensions. There will be less work for architects who design and engineers who erect skyscrapers... or for the restaurateurs, cab drivers, and small shops that service and live off big urban businesses.

Their retirement plans will need "re-engineering," a phrase all too current in Middle America....

7. Re-engineering the White Collar Workplace
A few years ago serious social commentators started using the phrase "re-engineering the corporation."

Prodded by the Japanese "lean production" approach, American companies launched an aggressive crusade to "downsize," trim, streamline, and compress traditional managerial hierarchy in their firms.

The Japanese method combines new management techniques with sophisticated machinery; the result is greater output with fewer resources and less labor. An MIT study in 1992 showed that at Toyota it takes 16 hours to build a car in less than 5 square feet of work space per vehicle, with less than 0.5% defects per car.

According to this study, GM takes over 30 hours per vehicle, using 8.15 square feet, with 1.3% defects. Toyota builds a car more quickly, with fewer defects, in less space, and with half the labor.

Toyota's competitive advantage is obvious.   One wonders how long our "Big Three" automakers will delay more rapid implementation of these Japanese methods. However gradually GM, Ford, and Chrysler awaken to the challenge, other American companies have already caught on.

"Deconstructing" their organizational hierarchies, eliminating middle management, compressing several jobs into a single process, they now speak of outsourcing as the eventual way to staff up for new projects.

Departments are being merged; divisions erased; paper flow minimized.   Networks or teams process information and compress decision-making time.

For example, at one time IBM Credit Corporation took seven days to process financing requests through five different departments and multiple clerks. Now "lean," IBM can do the process in four hours. One case worker handles the whole thing.

But the worker is not alone. He or she also has a computer that interfaces with multiple data bases. *The other case workers are out of a job.*

Another example is Wal-Mart. This retailing pioneer uses scanners to gather information at the point of sale; it transmits the data electronically to its suppliers; they ship directly to the stores. Purchase orders, bills of lading, on-hand inventories all become superfluous. *And so do the "middlemen" once needed to deal with orders, shipping, and warehousing.*

The revolution hitting the managerial class continues. Intel reduced its hierarchy of managers in some operations from ten to five. Kodak cut its management levels from 13 to four. In the spring of 1995 Mobil announced plans for worldwide cuts of over 4,000.

Intel, Kodak, and Mobil cut up and down their corporate hierarchy. It's not just the extra Minimum Wage employee in the mail room who gets the axe. Often it's 40-year-olds with impressive resumes -- and kids in college.

> **Some experts predict that re-engineering the economy could result in 20% unemployment in the next decade.**

In an earlier era an employee commonly put in 100,000 hours at the job over his lifetime. Now it is possible that he will put in as few as 50,000 hours at the job.

Unless they do something that *produces income with their unemployed time*, these refugees from "lean" corporations will not save much for retirement.

8. "Smart" Robots

The corollary to the "handwriting on the wall" about computers is this:

> **Whatever can be done electronically will not be done manually. Or, if a robot can do it, a human will not.**

Automakers rush to employ robots wherever they can. Mazda hopes to have its final assembly line 50% automated within five years. Companies no longer rely solely on hand-sculpted clay models of future car designs: "virtual reality" cars on computer screens can be produced in minutes; the older clay models took six weeks.

26

A small team of technicians can run new high-technology computerized steel mills. In a joint venture between Nippon Steel and Inland Steel, an automated cold rolling mill in northwest Indiana reduces production time from twelve days to *one hour*.

United States Steel employed 120,000 workers in 1980. By 1990 it was able to produce the same amount with only 20,000 workers. The next generation of "smart robots" will cause this number of workers to thin out even more.

In the rubber industry the story is the same. In 1995 Goodyear produced 30% more tires than in 1988, yet it employed 24,000 fewer employees. The difference was automation.

The chemical industry is no different. Productivity is increasing, but the number of personnel declined by 6% in the short period 1990 through mid-1992.

In electronics manufacturing new high-tech equipment can assemble circuit boards in half the time taken by the older system. Note: the *equipment* does the assembling. From 1981 to 1993, General Electric tripled its sales -- and *reduced* its worldwide workforce from 400,000 to less than 230,000.

AT&T announced replacement of 6,000 long-distance operators with voice-recognition technology. And voice-mail systems sharply reduce need for telephone receptionists. Efficiency improves: AT&T handles 50% more calls *with 40% fewer workers*.

Indeed, AT&T's shrinkage continued through 1995. A "News Release" to shareholders dated September 20, 1995, announced "Strategic Restructuring" for the 21st Century. The eighteenth paragraph stated:

"GIS [AT&T Global Information Solutions] -- which currently employs about 43,000 people in more than 120 countries -- also announced a major cost-cutting initiative that will lead to the elimination of approximately 8,500 jobs."

The pattern is clear: repetitive tasks, "mindless" activities, moving dead weight, data organization and transmission, etc. -- all can be handled by "smart" machines managed by few people.

In every instance, productivity gains are impressive. Better products and better services, frequently at lower cost, come out of the automated systems.

27

But at the same time, the avalanche of layoffs continues. And as the well-educated but newly unemployed technicians, managers, and supervisors scramble to come up with money for the mortgage, they wonder how they can save any money for retirement.

The clock keeps ticking.

9. Merger, Outsourcing: The "Virtual Company"

When one company swallows another, the digestion process causes job loss. Usually the takeover plan is simple: take the assets, but cut the overhead... i.e., prune the ranks of employees.

Every time there is a bank merger, umpty-ump jobs are lost.

Sometimes a merger looks like a marriage between equals. Even so, there are layoffs. When Lockeed and Martin-Marietta merged in 1995, Lockeed-Martin's new management announced plans to dismiss 25,000 employees.

Even if companies are not swallowed or merged, they keep looking for ways to minimize full-time employment. "Temp" personnel firms are growing rapidly, as many companies take on "contingent" workers.

A business engages these contractual workers for a day, a week, or longer -- even up to six months -- or it takes them on to deal with a particular task, contract, or project. This is "outsourcing."

It's the modern equivalent of marketplace hiring in ancient times: men go to the town square, stand around, and wait for someone to engage them for a day. No lasting commitments.

William Bridges' book, *Jobshift*, gives many cases where men and women who formerly worked full time for a big corporation -- with the usual package of health and retirement benefits -- now *are still engaged by them, working under contract* -- **and with no health and retirement benefits**.

Many firms now contract out research, production, and sales. The president of a Maryland company, Alpha 1 Biomedicals Inc., says that "infrastructure" -- buildings and workforce -- is not success; he says he suddenly realized that

> "Really, the only success in business is having a product. The question is, how do you limit risk? You do that by

28

limiting the stuff that's easy to build but hard to get rid of... like buildings and laboratories and big work forces."

These "lean" firms keep money otherwise absorbed by numerous employees and their security nets -- or remit part of it to the "temp" firm that screened, trained, and maintained the "contingent" employee on a roster of available people for short-notice tasks.

The ranks of potential "temp" workers keep growing. By mid-1995 it was possible to engage professionals, such as attorneys, on a "temp" basis. In 1993 and 1994 over one-third of college graduates could not find a "good job." Some became waiters; many worked as "temps."

Whenever supply outstrips demand, prices drop. The oversupply of these temporary workers is expanding. Demand for their services grows too, but -- because computers are replacing so many human tasks -- not as fast. Thus there is heavy downward pressure on temporary workers' wages.

As with most jobs, the person who gets the job is paid the average of what it takes to replace him. If you are a member of a group of 25 people willing to work for $7.50 an hour, to insist on $10.00 or $12.00 an hour is to get you nothing but unemployment. Zilch. Nada. One of the other 24 will get the -- temporary -- job.

For a formerly full-time worker, becoming a "temp" is a step backward, unless intangible benefits -- freedom to sleep late some mornings -- are seen as compensation. But financially, the average "temp" -- the Single Mom, the Between Jobs Junior Executive, the Graduate Student -- will not make enough to save for retirement.

A chapter in Jeremy Rifkin's landmark study, *The End of Work*, titled, "High-Tech Winners and Losers," recounts stories of more losers than winners. It discusses the plight of "the declining Middle," and punctuates social commentary with case after case of out-of-work middle management men in their 40s.

They wander around the wreckage of their careers like a dazed auto accident victim at the scene of the wreck.

They pore over the papers checking out job leads. They write, rewrite, and re-rewrite their resumes. They haunt libraries to read business publications. After awhile they watch more television... do household chores... go to support group meetings... or earn $6.00 per hour as a temp at H&R Block doing tax returns.

29

They no longer save for retirement. Dealing with the present is painful enough.

Some console themselves with the thought that at least they will have Social Security. The politicians of both parties promise that they will not "tinker with Social Security."

But as with so many other things Government promises to do for us citizens, there is less there than meets the eye....

CHAPTER 3:   SOCIAL INSECURITY

There are many oxymorons in the English language: *loud silence...
jumbo shrimp... honest politician.* The last has produced a new one:
Social Security.

****

A Carrot for a Short-Lived Horse

In 1900 the average person's lifespan was less than 50 years. So, as
Bismarck and other German social reformers of the 1870s must have
realized, to promise the citizens "security" at age 65 was to dangle a
carrot before a horse that would not live to eat it.

In 1935 the average person's lifespan was around 65 years.

Until the Depression most Americans worked into old age. And those
who could not work that long received care from their families. But in
1935 the public mood was ready to start redistributing the wealth. They
just didn't call it that.

The classic redistribution-of-wealth mentality works this way: "A"
and "B" get together to impose a tax on "C" so they can give his money
to "D", who out of a mix of envy of "C," gratitude to "A" and "B," and
selfishness, then votes for "A" and "B" again so they can repeat the
process next year.

"A" and "B" justify playing Robin Hood by claiming that "C" has
plenty of money and, in any event, has a social responsibility to help "the
needy." Of course, "D" is "needy."

Envy and selfishness not being quite as pervasive in the 1930s as
today, the Bismarcks of that decade had to claim -- and many of them

believed -- that the Social Security system was just a means of "forced savings."

That is, so all you "C's" out there would not fritter your money away on trivia, the Government would force you to "set aside" in "your own account" some of what you earned. Then, when you became a "D" in your retiring years, they would give it back to you.

Because we ordinary citizens -- or most of us -- tend to be improvident, they told us, the Congress, having a greater degree of thrift, providence, and proper sense of spending priorities, would make up for our moral/financial weakness.

It never seemed to dawn on them that you could do better by putting money into Whole Life insurance.

What will you get for your 40 years paying into the System? According to the Social Security Administration itself, your "Projected Primary Social Security Benefits" -- Maximum Monthly Benefits at Normal Retirement Age -- were these in 1988:

Age in 1988	Worker Alone	Worker & Spouse (Both 65)
65	$ 838	$1257
55	$1003	$1504
45	$1201	$1801
35	$1358	$2037

An article in *Worth* magazine (October, 1995), pointed out that if a hypothetical John and Mary paid in $465,187, and their employers chipped in another $465,187, they would get, after taxes and in constant 1995 dollars, after tax benefits of $358,070 when they retire in the year 2016.

If John and Mary handled the same money themselves, they would receive a slightly higher rate of interest... they could "borrow against" the cash value for pre-retirement needs like college or a new house... and the Government would not get its hands into their cookie jar and give the money to someone else.

As a matter of fact, if John and Mary had put the same money into an S&P 500 Index in 1972, earned a total return of 10% annually, and lost purchasing power by 4% per year, by the year 2016 they would have a retirement nest egg of $1,730,227 (in constant 1995 dollars).

The idea that Congress has a greater sense of thrift and proper priorities is a joke. But don't laugh! You and I cannot opt out of the system. So the joke's on us.

Besides that fiction, they told us another: that "The employer will pay one half," -- thus making the employer another "C" to give money to all those deserving "D's" out there.

Juggling the Books

This is a bookkeeping pretense.

In reality, the employer has only so much money he can spend on his workers: he pays them salary... or he also pays for fringe benefits. When he pays salary, they get it directly. When he spends on fringe benefits -- e.g., health insurance, retirement fund, etc. -- he has less to pay the workers in salary.

So the more the Government forces the employer to set aside for his workers, the less money he has to pay them directly. In this scheme, the Government forces a transfer from the workers, supposedly to give it back to them at retirement: take away money they could make *now*, and pay it to them *later*.

This scheme worked o.k. when there were 35 workers putting *in* for every one taking *out*; and when the Congress showed some of that foresight they pretend ordinary citizens do not have, and kept their fingers out of the cookie jar they made us contribute into.

They called the cookie jar, "The Social Security Trust Fund." You get the idea of a big pile of money in some bank vault somewhere. Not so.

The so-called Trust Fund has nothing in it, except I.O.U.'s from Congress. These are called "special public-debt obligations" (SPDOs) issued by the Treasury. To deal with immediate needs -- i.e., largely to give money to the "D's" of today who demand the most -- our frugal, provident Congress borrows from the Trust Fund.

Congress uses debt instruments, those SPDOs, its equivalent of promissory notes, to "replace" the funds it takes.

Congress now taxes you to generate immediate income. It pays that money out to current recipients of Social Security. So nothing goes into your "account"; Congress has spent it already.

Of course, they promise to pay the money back. They expect to get the money from future taxes.

Of Pyramids and Ponzi Schemes

This looks like a Ponzi scheme. Carlo Ponzi, you recall, created an "investment" scheme paying early excessive returns. For a while he pulled it off by paying the first wave of investors "dividends" out of the recruitment fees from the second wave, then paying the second wave out of the recruiting fees deposited by the third wave, and so on.

The scheme relies on an infinite growing pool of new investors; if the number of humans willing to hand their money over to a con man were infinite, Ponzi might still be in business. The illegal "pyramid" works only if there is an endless chain of new recruits.

Right now, however, it seems only ignorance and stupidity are near infinite. The number of paying *people* is finite -- whether paying to Ponzi or paying taxes to Congress.

Unfortunately, the pool of tax-payers is not only finite, **it is shrinking**, compared to the **growing** number of "tax-payees."

In 1950, there were 16 active workers paying into the system for each inactive retiree who drew benefits. Today there are less than five and some writers say it is down to three. In 2030, there will be barely two workers to support one retiree.

This means that if both husband and wife work, *the two of them will have a third adult to maintain*: a stranger who, they will quickly conclude, should support himself.

Between 2015 and 2030, Social Security will collapse. Ponzi ran out of people who would "invest" in his scheme. Old people will run out of young people willing to transfer their income to old people.

Life Expectancy

The problem is a mix of demographics and medical advances.

The "Baby Boomers" are moving through time like a pig swallowed by a boa constrictor. The "bulge" is now in the middle years and soon, inevitably, will be in the elder years.

The fertility rate is now below the population replacement level of 2.1 births per woman. It is falling further. In the next 20 years it will move

34

down to 1.9. The workers retiring are not being replaced by enough workers working.

Meantime, life expectancy has *increased by an extra 30 years in only a century*. In 1900 it was 46 years for men and 48 years for women. In 1935, it was 60 for men and 63 for women. Today it is in the high 70s. Soon it will be over 80.

Men 46 were still vigorous and could still work the farm. Today, despite medical advances, men 76 are not vigorous enough, in most cases, to work the farm -- or other high-stress, competitive jobs.

In 1945 there were only 771,000 people collecting Social Security. Today we have more than 35,000,000. The Social Security Administration estimates that by the year 2045, there will be 72,000,000 -- that's nearly 100 times *more* people receiving benefits than in 1945... yet the population of the U.S. will have scarcely tripled.

Further, since Social Security taxes are based on wages earned, when wages drop, so do the "contributions" of the workers. But American wage growth is not only stagnant, it is in retreat. From 1973 to 1994 real wages fell at an average rate of one percent per year.

This means that the backbone of a free society, the Middle Class, has lost 20% of its purchasing power in two decades. People were already going backwards even before the ripples of corporate "downsizing" since 1985 kicked in.

The Social Security Board of Trustees' *Annual Report* produced a "best estimates" forecast: to maintain benefits at current levels would absorb between 25.78% and 30.21% of taxable payroll.

After those sums disappeared from your earnings, then IRS and the State tax people will show up at the door and demand *their* pound of flesh for income taxes.

In other words, Social Security taxes plus income taxes could easily take 60% of your income. Some analysts figure it will be closer to 75-80%.

This does not make sense. No one is going to work three weeks out of each month to give money to an old person they do not know, while both spouses and the teenage children have to work -- just to put bread on the table and gas in the car.

The Likely "Solution"

Something has to give. The grumbling among younger taxpayers over the Government's mandated Ponzi Scheme grows. As it gets louder, Congress will do something.

It will take a King Solomon to come up with a fair solution. And Congress is not populated with Solomons.

However, it will probably try to do what Solomon did when two women claimed the same baby: split the difference; offer to give each one half.

A Solomonic solution could "work," after a fashion, since Congress is splitting dollars, not babies. But the "difference" it will probably "split," will be this: (a) raise taxes and (b) lower benefits. Don't be surprised if Congress does both.

This tactic may get Congress off the hot seat. But the "cure" may kill the patient.

Remember, the patient is you and me and millions of other Americans. The goal is financial health in retirement: enough money to meet reasonable needs.

If Congress raises taxes, you and I have even less to save for retirement. If it lowers benefits, it means we have even less *in* retirement. If it does both, the retirees and would-be retirees suffer more -- and sooner.

The precedent is already there: since 1981, Congress has, one way or another, *cut* Social Security benefits seven times.

Oh yes, they tell the senior citizens that "Social Security is not on the table," and "We won't tinker with Social Security." But during President Clinton's first two years Congress passed a tax bill which, among other things, *taxed* some Social Security benefits: they did tinker.

Let's call a spade a spade. When you tax income, you lower the net of what one has to spend. Since *cash flow* is what people want, not "gross income *before* taxes"... and the tax *reduced* the cash flow... Congress managed to square the circle: they kept (gross) benefits the same but they also cut them to a (lower) net.

When you lower someone's cash flow... you reduce his purchasing power... and thus lower his standard of living.

Medicare and Medicaid and Medigap

A word on old-age health problems is appropriate here. These are real and the cost of dealing with them is also out of hand.

As I write this Congress is struggling with the problem. Whether they can fix it is anybody's guess.

"Cost containment" is one battle cry. That's governmentspeak for cutting the physicians' income.

Government is skilled at transferring a burden from one group to another. Physicians are a current target. Last year, when Blue Cross of Maryland obtained State permission to cut by 12% the amount they pay doctors for certain medical procedures, the State effectively cut their incomes by 12%.

But other costs are not so easily reduced by simple edict. One such is the growing expense of long-term care and nursing homes.

According to the U.S. House of Representatives Select Committee on Aging, over 50% of all long-term care costs are paid out of *private, personal resources*.

In 1965, the average nursing home cost for one year was $2,900. Today, it has increased by 1,200 percent! By the year 2001, the one year's average cost of nursing home care will be around $48,200.

> **Today's price tag of $3,000 per month or $36,000 per year is an amount higher than the average American's annual income.**

It is almost certain that the "snapshot" of these costs will blur with inflation over the next ten, twenty, or more years. If the cost is $36,000 per year in 1996, the price tag will say something over $60,000 -- maybe as high as $72,000 -- in 2006.

Again, "Mugged by the Rule of 72."

How will Americans take care of their elderly Mom and Dad in ten years? How will we take care of *ourselves* in twenty or thirty years?

It is easy to say, "They'll just have to keep on working." But for most people, such advice is unrealistic. They may not have the desire. They may not have the skills. There will be fewer jobs anyway. They may not have the stamina to compete with people half their age.

37

They *may not have good enough health* to keep on working.

Private charity is a partial answer that our country must begin to encourage. Every church will need to set up volunteer groups and special funding to care for its elderly.

But unfortunately, we can't all move in with the Little Sisters of the Poor.

This brings us to...

The Real Social Security Solution

On the macrocosmic -- national -- policy level, the only solution lies in imitating what Chile has done: privatize.

But on the microcosmic -- personal -- strategy level... that is, on *your and my level* of activity... protecting ourselves and our future... individually... the real solution lies in the program explained in the second half of this book.

It is also a form of "privatization." We just don't call it that.

"The Eleventh Commandment is: 'Thou Shalt Not Fool Thyself.'"

> **America has fooled itself into believing that Government, which has only the money it takes from its citizens, could provide them unlimited security.**

Even if Government did not charge a high "administrative fee," giving the problem to Government does not create any more money to deal with the problem than if the people kept their own problems and their own money to themselves.

Are we now smart enough to admit how stupid we've been?

Americans fooled themselves into thinking that they could endlessly transfer money from those who are working to those who are not, even though the first group shrinks and the second expands.

When will we stop violating the Eleventh Commandment?

Equally important to *you and me*: it is time to admit we fooled ourselves into handing over to strangers in the world's most profligate institution -- the United States Federal Government -- the responsibility for the health and security of everyone age 65 to 90 or beyond.

It's time to take our future into our own hands.

Besides a clarion call to everyone to "Do it yourself," there is another reason to go that route: *there is no other option.*

The Welfare State is collapsing. No longer can the magician pull the rabbits from the hat: there aren't any rabbits left in there. No longer can Government pull money out of an empty bank.

Like downtown buildings shaking in a major earthquake, the Welfare State is crumbling. Either it must be dismantled systematically, and its responsibilities transferred back to the people, or it collapses completely. Delay will only maximize the pain.

Big institutions -- the mega-bloated Federal Government, the bloated State Governments, huge erstwhile paternalistic corporations, big cities with countless payrollers -- all are running out of money.

Governments can no longer take from the so-called "rich," and give to the "deserving" poor. There are too few of the former, too many of the latter.

The United States Government has a *negative net worth.* If you or I went into a Bank, applied for a loan, and presented a balance sheet that looks like our national government's, the Bankers would toss us out on our ears -- if they didn't first rupture a blood vessel laughing.

Our national debt -- over four trillion dollars -- is more than all the money in circulation in the whole country. They could tax us 100% and they still couldn't pay the thing off.

They may try to escape -- temporarily -- by running the printing presses. Create fiat money. (*Fiat* is a Latin word which means, "Let it be." It's what God said when He created the universe.)

If you and I printed money, the Feds would throw us in the State Pen for counterfeiting. But when the Federal Reserve does it, with the acquiescence of Congress, it's "monetary policy."

If Congress allows this ploy, we will witness a rerun of Germany in 1923: hyper inflation, daily price jumps, the end of everyone's savings.

Congress will have to cut welfare benefits. They will cut Social Security. At least indirectly. They will tax it... and they will raise the age when you qualify to get it... and they will inflate the money so that what you do get doesn't buy as much.

The Welfare State is dead in the water. It's time to jump ship. Man the lifeboats.

We started with an oxymoron. "Social Security." But there's another phrase that is *not* an oxymoron.

Self-Reliance. **Produce your own retirement income: run your own business.**

CHAPTER 4:   BACK TO THE FUTURE

"To succeed in business, you need a product
or service which people want, need, and can
afford....   I would rather have 1% of the
work of each of 100 men than 100% of my
own work."
                              -- J.Paul Getty

****

By the year 2000, America will have come full circle. We started as
a nation of small businesses. From World War I to the close of the
Vietnam War, we were in an industrial/institutional phase, in which
working for a corporation, "the Job," seemed to be the road to freedom
and security. But today freedom and security, by that route, is only a
mirage. Indeed, the permanent Job, like distant desert water, itself is a
mirage.

For the country as a whole, there is only one option left: once again
to become a nation of small businesses.

For the erstwhile Job-holder whose job suffered "reduction in force"...
streamlining... downsizing... corporate restructuring... or any other
synonym for being laid off, there is only one way out: start a business
of your own.

Some people are like a driver whose car is out of gas: we stand
roadside, stare at the machine, deny the tank is empty, tell it to start again
when the key is turned.

But there's no point in bemoaning the past; it's time to start walking.
The sooner we accept reality the quicker we can move on.

The question is: which direction?

41

There are three possibilities: a conventional small business; a franchise; or an unconventional marketing business.

Conventional Small Business

A decade ago two stockbrokers in our town, fed up with the rat race, changed careers: they left their firm and opened a small hardware store in the neighborhood shopping center.

They had to deal with the four challenges of every start-up venture: time... money... knowledge... risk.

Time.   To show a profit, their neighborhood store was open from 10:00 a.m. to 9:00 p.m. Monday through Friday, from 8:00 a.m. to 5:00 p.m. on Saturdays, and at least six hours on Sundays. Seventy hours a week.

To make it work, the owners were there most of these hours, or they hired a reliable manager whom they had to pay enough to motivate him to stay reliable.

Money. The owners of the new venture leased space for 3-5 years; purchased insurance; paid electric, heat, and water charges. They put in extensive inventory and a computer with program to manage it. They bought a cash register/computer, which cost a few thousand dollars. They obtained "merchant status" with a bank, to process VISA and MC. They needed shelving and, being a hardware store, equipment, such as machines to mix paint and make keys.

Start-up costs can go to many tens of thousands of dollars.   The owners will obtain this money from their own savings or by personal loans.   Either way, there is expense involved: they lose interest their savings could have generated, or they pay interest to the lenders. It is not uncommon for an entrepreneur to mortgage his own home for start-up capital.

Until they open, their business makes no money.   But planning becomes nearly a full time endeavor. Thus they work without being paid. The loans -- from whatever source -- put bread and butter on the table. But in due time they must be repaid too.

Money is a constant concern.

Knowledge. How to run a small business is not taught in college. If a person does not have a father or brother under whose tutelage he can learn, he must be self-taught... in the School of Hard Knocks.

42

Most small business beginners are shocked to find that filling out paperwork takes the equivalent of one day per week. If they don't know basic bookkeeping, they hire an Accountant. If they need advice on business structure, whether and how to use a Corporation, a Limited Partnership, or a Limited Liability Company, they hire an Attorney.

In either case, they exchange money which they need for knowledge which they also need. This is a wise trade, since a small mistake made early can compound to a big problem later; but it is costly.

Business acumen results from experience. The sole proprietor cannot approach his competitor a block away for guidance on how best organize his store... hire assistants... advertise... promote special sales... deal with suppliers... anticipate market trends... use "loss leaders"... and dozens of other decisions which can mean the difference between profit and loss.

So, like a person entering a dark room, he must grope his way carefully, lest he trip. Even with care, ignorance of some fundamental may cost him dearly -- and perhaps cause the enterprise to fail.

Risk. The new businessman has "tied up" in the venture thousands of dollars which he can ill afford to lose. He also has hundreds, eventually thousands, of hours of his life invested as well -- time which he can never recapture.

The two stockbrokers' hardware store closed after five years in our area. I am not sure why, save that there was a small competitor only a block away, and two large discount-type hardware stores within five miles.

But it may have simply been overhead: one Saturday afternoon in August, I entered the store to buy a tube of caulk; the 100° heat coupled with the western sun against their windows strained the air conditioner, two clerks stood around the empty store, earning perhaps $6.00 per hour, and their only sale that hour may have been a $3.50 tube of caulk.

Starting a full-time one-location conventional small business is not the best route to take: three out of four will fail in the first five years.

Franchising

In the U.S. there are over 2,500 franchise systems. These have in excess of 534,000 franchise units, which represent only 3.2% of total businesses, yet *control over 34% of all retail and service revenue in the American economy.*

43

Not all franchises are created equal. Everyone can name a franchise which is successful: McDonalds. Few people know much about the ones which are less than successful.

The "upside" of a good franchise system is that you plug into an already proven system. People think you are "buying a franchise," but actually you invest your assets in a system to utilize the brand name, operating system, and ongoing support.

The desire to "be my own boss" is *not* fully satisfied by a franchise. A franchisee cannot think of himself as an independent "owner." If he does so, he will be tempted to try to change the system. (Notice: McDonalds does not sell hot dogs; the famous arches are never red or blue: the home office does not permit anyone to tinker with their formula.)

> **The franchisee owns the assets of his own franchise, but he is licensed only to run someone else's business system.**

The desire to become a franchisee is grounded on belief that he can be more successful using someone else's brand, and operating according to their methods, than he could if he opened up his own independent business and competed against them.

Compared to setting up a *conventional* business of one's own, the advantages of franchising include:

> opening more quickly... developing a profitable customer base faster... having less risk... national advertising presence... built-in name recognition... strong support system you can call upon for advice... readily identifiable trade name and goodwill associated with it... centralized, collective buying power.

Disadvantages of franchising usually include:

> frequently substantial up-front entry fee... high continuing advertising and royalty fees (5-10% of gross profit is not uncommon)... loss of personal control... need to quit your full-time job... being "locked in" to suppliers chosen by the franchisor... inability to will your business to wife and children... one-sided agreement drafted by franchisor that may not fully protect your territory and interests....

44

Adding It All Up

Considering time, money, knowledge, and risk, franchising is often superior to a conventional business: the risk is usually less and it does provide a proven system coupled with home-office guidance.

But it takes a complete break with one's past career and one's current income.

To finesse this problem a franchisee may act as an investing partner and let someone else handle day-to-day management. However, this approach is a mixed bag: the franchisee ties up big money but loses control; and the hired manager has the daily headaches but knows he's building someone else's business.

The best aspect of a franchise is availability of knowledge: one does not "reinvent the wheel." The worst aspect is cost: payments to the franchisor add substantial overhead.

The franchise system has enabled many entrepreneurs to create strong retirement security and, in some cases, build real wealth. But most doctors, lawyers, dentists, and other professionals -- as well as job-at-risk middle management executives in this era of "downsizing" -- need a better way.

For the millions of victims of the Economic Revolution hitting the "retirement crunch," franchising is too costly... takes too much time... requires a burn-the-bridges-behind-me commitment... *and may not produce enough surplus income to deal with retirement needs anyway.*

What they need is the best of both worlds: a way to generate *full-time* income though working only *part time*... a system that produces *residual* income that keeps coming in although one's advancing age eventually prevents putting in much -- or any -- time.

Fortunately, some of the very market forces which caused corporate downsizing created new business forms that can meet retirement needs.

Institutional Joint Ventures

More and more companies are entering forms of innovative cooperation with outside marketers. Reducing their own in-house personnel has prompted them to enter strategic business alliances or *joint ventures in which two or more business entities help each other.*

Some examples:

- A few months ago, my Shell gas credit car bill contained flyers offering pen sets, small watches, and... *bird houses.*

  "Bird houses!" I exclaimed to my wife. "Doesn't Shell have any pride? A company their size -- marketing *bird houses*!"

But *I* was wrong, not Shell. It makes sense to have the bird house company pay to mail a month's billings -- in return for getting access to tens of thousands of Shell customers.

- Citibank VISA markets American Airlines "frequent flyer miles." Sign up for *this* Bank's VISA card, they importune, and for every dollar you run across the card, you get "miles." So you can spend your way into some free airline trips.

Both American Airlines and Citibank win: each gets free advertising among the other's customers. Each captures your motivation to use the other's service and often turns it into a motive to use its own service.

- NationsBank has introduced a VISA card in cooperation with Blockbuster Video. Same idea. Sign up on the card and get six free video rentals. Use the card and get more free rentals.

- McDonalds and Coca-Cola collaborate. McDonalds has 17,000 outlets around the world. Merely through its joint venture with Big Mac, Coca-Cola reaches more thirsty mouths daily than the U.S. Army.

There are many other examples of institutional joint ventures. In all cases, like a halfback behind a blocking lineman, aggressive companies seeking expanded market share run "behind" another firm which has already penetrated a market segment and, using its "blocking," reach places and people they could not have reached alone.

But the more farsighted companies are going beyond even that. They have come to realize that *any person* can be a "profit center" or "marketing outlet"....

Joint Ventures *with Individuals*

Since 1980, and intensifying since the Recession of the last half dozen years, three powerful trends have converged.

First, threatened by corporate layoffs, highly capable men and women are looking for ways to diversify their income. They realize they can no longer rely on only one source of income. Quite a few ask themselves,

> "Why go back to a corporation, even if I can find one to hire me, and risk being cut by the same layoff axe in a couple years? Why not become an Independent Contractor?"

Second, not everyone laid off was "dead wood." When companies cut their ranks by tens of thousands, they also cut thousands who were productive. They need to hang on to the productivity of the people they did not keep. So they started scrambling to find Independent Contractors to reach their market.

Third, the electronic revolution -- computer, modem, fax, and phone -- enable small, part-time businesses *with few or no employees* to compete "on a level playing field" with anyone in the world.

Some of the smartest businessmen in the world have found a unique way to harness these trends to their advantage.

New Corporate Strategy

The following transcript has been changed enough to protect individual anonymity; thus modified, it is a composite of many discussions in corporate board rooms in the last five years.

Scene: Executive Committee meeting of a multi-billion-dollar company. The Chief Executive Officer and four top VPs are discussing how to maintain market share while trimming personnel.

CEO: "Gentlemen, our plans to downsize by 25,000 more are well along. This action will mean substantial cuts in company cars, regional offices, pension costs, and Social Security payments. It will save us over $2 billion this year alone."

VP#1: "Chief, it's a good strategy. That money can go to R&D and we'll have some left to pay down our debt. But we still need a way to move our product into our worldwide markets -- without all those employees we've let go."

VP#2: "Right, and my Alternative Marketing Committee has come up with a way to 'Eat our cake and have it too.' We can engage people as Independent Contractors. No more W-2s and expense account headaches."

CEO: "I'm open-minded to anything that will expand our market share without big costs. But I don't want the Personnel Department 'tail' to wag the corporate 'dog.' The last thing we need is having to contract with another 25,000 people...."

VP#2: "Chief, may I present a quick briefing on a relatively new approach called 'Network Marketing'?"

CEO: "Sure. We captured our market share by being on the cutting edge of change. New ideas don't scare me."

VP#2: "Chief, we can take advantage of the very social and economic changes that forced us to restructure and lay off so many people in the first place.

"The problem was overhead. It cost almost $100,000 for every middle manager who earned $60,000. And because the corporate bureaucracy hid half of them, we had a terrible time measuring their productivity.

"Now, imagine a system where we deal with an association of independent contractors, field reps, marketing associates -- offer them good pay *whenever they move our product* but *nothing* when they don't. Pay them cash, use 1099s, let them handle their own expenses.

"This is like the outsourcing we now use for many of our short-term projects. It's better for lots of reasons: for one, when they work for a separate Personnel Corporation which is under contract to us, if they get fired, they can't sue us.

"At any rate, since the early 1960s a few companies, usually in consumables like cosmetics, vitamins, food supplements, personal and home care products, have bypassed stores and salaried salesmen. Instead, they assembled a field network of private individuals.

"Call it *referral-based* or *interactive* marketing. It uses word-of-mouth advertising. This saves a ton of money. It omits 'middlemen' like wholesales and retailers. About 70% of most retail cost is due to our country's complex distribution process. Most of that money can go toward discounts and monetary incentives to find other marketing associates.

"Discounts, usually between 30% and 50%, create brand loyalty, since their people save money; and income potential for those who want to buy at wholesale and sell at retail.

48

"Then -- and here is the real genius of the system -- they use the remainder of the 70% for bonuses to any representative who 'builds a network' by bringing in other people who want to do the same thing.

"Can you imagine the money they save in interview and training costs alone? Independent field reps, not company employees, handle interviews. The company does not pay for interviewing and training. The independent rep's incentive to recruit and help new people get up to speed is a share of company profit as the new field rep generates sales.

"Some network marketing companies have 50,000, or 100,000, or even a couple hundred thousand active field reps. They don't pay Social Security or other benefits. Their people are independent contractors -- part-timers -- who work -- or don't -- when they want.

"What makes some work hard is the high income they can make. The best companies pay very well. It is possible for a committed marketing rep to earn a six figure income -- *part time.*

"This happens because typically their incentive system rewards their reps both for the sales of persons they recruit... and it *also* pays a percent of corporate income from sales generated by people 'down' many 'levels.'

"For example: A brings in B, C, and D... and each brings in five active people... and each of those recruits another five, and so on down six levels. At that point there are over 1,800 people in A's organization. It looks something like a tree: trunk, branches, limbs... with each leaf standing for an individual. And A makes money not only from his own sales. He makes a small percentage of the sale price of product that flows through the businesses of all the others."

CEO: "Let me interrupt. I have a few questions. First, this idea sounds brilliant -- but if it's so good, why didn't the MBAs among our senior people put it in front of the Executive Committee a long time ago?"

VP#3: "Sir, the answer has three parts. First, the MBAs come out of grad school filled with academic theory, whereas this is a grass-roots, practical approach to marketing.

"Second, when Network Marketing started, only a minority of people took it seriously, partly because mostly unsophisticated types tried it. But today many major corporations are looking for shortcuts to extra income and there are plenty of professional people involved.

"Third, we as a company did not need this -- or we thought we didn't -- as long as we were fat and sassy with plenty of extra in-house personnel. But today we have to run lean; we need outsiders to help.

CEO: "O.K. That makes sense. Times change. What might seem eccentric 20 or 30 years ago could become mainstream today.... Next question: what kinds of products go through these 'networks'?"

VP#4: "Chief, as far as we can tell, just about *anything*, from satellite dishes to shower soap... from coffee to cosmetics... from stocks and insurance to pre-paid legal protection... from voice mail and long distance phone service to water filters. In fact, as far as I can see, *everything* you and I use in our own homes, except perhaps carpets and wallpaper, is marketed through these networks."

VP#2: "The only things that would not profitably be handled, I guess, are really big things like pianos... and highly perishable items like bananas and ice cream."

CEO: "Are you saying, then, that *our* company's product lines can be moved through a Network Marketing system?"

VP#3: "No doubt about it. And we'll probably get more results by harnessing the ambition of thousands of people who are moved more by unlimited incentives than flat salaries.

VP#2: "Also, as we restructure, we're turning to outside contractors for services traditionally done in-house. We save on fringe benefits. All the Network Marketing approach does is to take this trend a step further: we can contract with independent outsiders to market for us. Call it a '*virtual marketing department*'!"

CEO: [Smiling] "Before you launch us into cyberspace, give me some down-to-earth answers to two basic questions: just *how* and *why* does this system work?"

VP#2: "In my opinion, it's America-come-full-circle. Sir, remember when you were a kid? You grew up in a small town. The shop owners often lived above or behind their own stores. Marketing was face-to-face *by people who knew each other as friends*, often for years...."

CEO: "...My grandfather was a jeweler. I still recall the four-room apartment he and my grandmother had over their store."

VP#2: "Right. And probably when he repaired the setting on a neighbor's diamond ring, or fixed someone's watch, sometimes he walked it over to their house to take it back to them."

VP#3: "Most small town merchants delivered. In fact, even in the big cities back in the 1940s, the milkman, the baker, the local grocery store -- they all delivered right to your door. And the 'General Store' was a place you could buy everything from fishing equipment to raincoats to pots and kettles."

CEO: "They all knew each other. 'Credit' was a personal accommodation between the store owner and maybe the town mechanic or dentist -- not a piece of plastic issued by a Bank a thousand miles away.

"Today it's mega-malls, warehouse-size stores, clerks nowhere to be seen -- depersonalization. And everybody in such a hurry that face-to-face service, between friends, like in my granddad's day -- well, that's history."

VP#2: "History can repeat itself. With proper electronic adjustments, of course. We've all heard the phrase, 'Old wine in new bottles.'"

CEO: "I see where you're going. Network Marketing brings back personal service... in-home delivery... the possibility of a friendship relationship between merchant and customer."

VP#1: "It's possible to have a 'shopping mall without walls': the marketing associate offers his customers an 800 number for ordering -- actually, it will soon be possible to bypass the phone: the man or woman marketing will be able to use a CD-ROM and computer for interactive ordering. In a short time, maybe two, three years, customers will be savvy enough on a computer to do their own ordering."

VP#2: "Technology is driving the marketplace back to the home."

VP#4: "So each independent marketer has his own 'General Store,' with no capital investment and maybe not much actual inventory. His 'upline' supplements what he does have, and telephone, computer, and fax give him access to suppliers all over the country."

VP#2: "Whether it's one product line or hundreds, through independent marketers a company can educate customers to the process of using telephone and computer to order from their own homes -- and let UPS worry about the icy roads in winter."

CEO: "Instead of stacking our products only in empty stores, where a customer can never find a minimum-wage clerk who would know how to 'sell' him on any special benefits, we could also have independent marketers *with an 'equity position' in the sales process itself*: they'd get a share of the profit much larger than an hour's flat wage."

VP#1: "And we'd be riding the sociological trend-wave: people are 'cocooning'; they don't want to spend Saturday and most of Sunday shopping. A lot of them would like it if our marketing associates delivered, like in your grandfather's day.

"There's another wave, too: many people are looking for ways to supplement their income part-time. I don't want to sound insensitive, but some of them are the people that 'corporate restructuring' had to lay off.

"Anyway, the 'equity position' you mention can be quite lucrative: they share in the profit not only from their own sales but from all the sales in their 'network.'"

CEO: "That reminds me of the first question: how do we do this without having to contract with 25,000 separate individuals?"

VP#2: "Two possibilities. First, we set up a small Personnel Corporation and it hires a few Network Marketing experts who try to build a network for us. Or, second, we go out and find an already established Network Marketing company and get our products into their network."

CEO: "We'll have to study that. But my first instinct is that it makes no sense to reinvent the wheel. Why don't you and your team identify two or three top companies that do business this way and we'll propose a joint venture to them.

"Anyway, I can see the advantages to a manufacturer like ourselves. But I'd like you to outline what the benefits are to the field reps or, let's call them, distributors of our products. Legitimate self-interest is the strongest of all motives. All these independent contractors are not in love with our corporation -- or any other. They are in love with their own families and their own future.

"So -- since we're out of time for this meeting -- send me a Memorandum listing, *from the view point of an individual who wants to earn money*, the reasons he should get into network marketing."

CHAPTER 5: VERY GOOD AND QUITE TRUE

> "Just because you don't recognize a good business when you see one doesn't mean you didn't see one."
> -- John Sestina, CFP

****

Memorandum on Network Marketing

The unique system of Network Marketing has so many advantages over conventional stores, franchises, sole proprietorships, and most professional practice, that it will become the primary distribution system in this country in the next five to ten years.

Here are twenty reasons why Network Marketing is better than any other form of business.

(1)   Low Investment.

In most programs, a person can start his marketing business for less than $250.00. Since this outlay is a tax-deductible business expense, the out-of-pocket is 15% - 33% less.

Also, usually a marketing associate is authorized to buy the company's products or services at wholesale.

Sometimes savings in the first three months will equal or exceed the cost of starting the business: i.e., *he started a business for no cost at all!*

(2)   No Boss

When a person is an independent contractor he cannot be fired. To the question, "If you could make the same amount of money running your own business as you earn working for someone else, which would you rather do?" over 80% answer: "Work for myself!"

53

When a person works in a team of independent contractors, he gets the benefit of the group dynamics and leadership from seniors, as he would in a corporation, *without being under the corporate "we-own-you" authority/control structure.*

If the marketing associate does not drink too deeply of the heady wine of freedom, he can enjoy the best of both worlds: access to a mentor system of guidance from the leadership while being his own boss.

(3)   Working From Home

The daily commute to the 30-story concrete-and-glass filing cabinet has lost its appeal. But most corporate managers and big law firm attorneys still spend much of their lives on highways and in parking garages.

A growing group of entrepreneurs would rather work from home. A network marketing business is *designed* for such a setting: being totally decentralized, it does not need 50,000 square feet of floor space. A back bedroom will do.

This means no extra costs of lease, insurance, electricity, furniture, or computer. Except for modest record-keeping and maybe a software program, virtually none of the "overhead" expenses of a conventional business. And no commute.

(4)   Fewer, Flexible Hours

People are too busy. The big newsmagazines like *Time* and *Newsweek* carry stories which tell how trying to find *time* is what bedevils Americans in the 90s. Two, three, and even *four* job families are now commonplace.

The Working Poor are not alone on the treadmill. There are plenty of doctors, lawyers, CPAs, and other professionals who, at age 45, want to throw in the towel, quit the rat race, and buy a one-way ticket to Maine, there to open an inn.

A person in a full-time job or profession cannot toss it all overboard and charge willy-nilly into a different career. He needs to develop it "on the side," while keeping his regular work to pay his regular bills.

But a Network Marketing business is *essentially* part time. Business activity can be squeezed in at lunch, for a few hours in the evening, or any time on the weekend.

(5)   Time-Compounding through Duplication

Tom Monahan owns Domino's Pizza. Around 30 years ago he had one pizza place. He cooked all the pizza himself. And he did not make much money. Today Mr. Monahan has about 5,000 pizza outlets. He does not cook any pizza. But he gets a share of the money produced by *other people* cooking pizza in 5,000 different places.

The Kroc family controls McDonalds. Though deceased, Ray Kroc earns more money than any ten living JDs, PhDs, or CPAs that I know. With 17,000 restaurants around the world, McDonalds -- not Mrs. Kroc -- produces, as their signs say, "Billions and Billions."

You thought the signs meant Burgers. Perhaps. But it's possible the signs also mean Dollars.

While the doctors, dentists, attorneys, accountants, and others do all the "cooking" themselves in their fields, Tom Monahan and Ray Kroc brilliantly *duplicated themselves* thousands of times and took a small percent, as Getty advised, of the work of each of thousands of people. On a small scale and with virtually no overhead, Network Marketing does the same thing.

(6)   Minimal Legal Liability

A corporation or sole proprietor businessman can be liable for the misdeeds of his employees in the ordinary course of business. This is called "vicarious liability."

The "Employer-Employee" relation inherently threatens the Employer: every Employee can create liability for the Employer by doing something in the course of employment which falls below the legal standard of care. In terms of legal risk, to employ 20 people can create more exposure to lawsuits than to sponsor, directly or through others, a network of 2,000 independent people.

The Network Marketing relationship is different. No person in a downline can, *just by virtue of that relation*, create vicarious liability for his sponsor. No one is "Principal" or "Agent." This is true even if the association includes tens, hundreds, even thousands of other Independent Contractors.

(7)   No Special Licenses or Training to Join

To become an Attorney, a person must go to law school for three years.   Then, in most States, he or she must also pass the Bar Examination.

The direct cost of those years -- tuition, books, travel -- can rise to well over $100,000. Indirect costs -- for example, the opportunity foregone to earn salary in some job -- could be another $30,000 to $100,000 or more over that time.

So *just to start a Law Business*, a person might be "in the hole" upwards of $200,000, before seeing his first paying client.

To become a Doctor, the training takes longer. By and large, the costs are even higher.

A good Network Marketing business has none of these excessive costs. A Law Business or a Medical Business costs thousands and thousands of dollars just to enter. That's "overhead in advance."

But the mark of a good business is *not* overhead. It is profit. "Advance overhead," which must be recouped before a person can be said to earn any profit -- thus before any *net* income -- is only a drawback.

In the race toward funding retirement, the doctor and the attorney start a couple hundred thousand dollars "in the hole." Network Marketing has no holes.

(8)   No Discrimination

In the ideal society, men and women would advance on merit alone. They would be paid what they're worth. They would prove what they are worth -- by performance on an objective scale, not by race, ethnic background, sex, religion or nepotism.

Network Marketing rewards a person not because of color or gender, homeland or faith. If Joan sells more product and sponsors more people who in turn sell and sponsor, than does Tom, Dick, or Harry, then it does not matter if Joan is black or female, from Turkey or Peru. It makes no difference if she's Catholic, Jewish, Muslim, or Zoroastrian.

Joan will make more money than Tom, Dick, or Harry. There is no "glass ceiling." The company or companies she represents probably do not even know whether she is Hispanic or Asian, plain or beautiful, old or young. And *they don't care.*

Joan does not have to worry about the color or gender or age, etc., of her co-workers or her sponsor. They cannot fire her. As long as she's honest, neither can the company.

(9)   Tax Benefits

A salaried employee has no tax benefits related to the job. He cannot deduct his commute to and from work. Nor lunch. Nor use of personal den for work brought home from the office.

The average American with a job has only one serious deduction: the interest on one's home mortgage.

As a business, Network Marketing enables a person to claim many legitimate business expense deductions. These include home office, payments to children for actual work, travel to presentations, seminars and business conferences even if at vacation resorts.

(10)   No Employees

In Network Marketing, no one is employed by a company or by any senior person. One works "with" but not "for" an interrelated group of like-minded independent contractors.

No Employees means no one for whom to pay Social Security, no one to hire or fire, no problems trying to decide whom to promote, no maze of rules from EEOC, OSHA, CPSC.

No Employees means no money spent while groping for motivational techniques to get the lazy ones moving.

No Employees means no worries about insurance for those who work late, liability for their torts while on a business errand, or watching who has access to the cash register.

Long before big companies started to "outsource," every person in Network Marketing was doing it.

(11)   No Risk

The entry cost is trivial. The time investment is equally small: just a few hours per week, not enough to detract from being a practicing dentist, high-billable-hours attorney, or full-time truck driver.

Best of all, the network marketer risks little time -- and *none of his regular job income.* Giving up bowling, golf, one's basement room hobby, or prime time TV for a couple years for a return of a five-to-six-figure lifetime income is not anything risked; it's plain old common sense.

(12)   No Accounts Receivable and Collection Headaches.

The "Bottom Line" does not sneak up and swallow the "Top Line." Many professionals such as doctors and dentists do the work -- and then, as patients, insurance companies, Blue Cross, and others haggle over what is "covered," wait months to get paid.

Network Marketing businesses are normally "cash-and-carry." One does not tie up capital; efforts do not go uncompensated.

(13)   Inexpensive, Sometimes Free, Training.

The basic academic training in the major professions costs tens of thousands of dollars.   Then, as one goes on in the fields of Law, Accounting, Dentistry, Insurance, and Medicine, most States require "continuing education."   Often the cost comes to hundreds, indeed thousands, of added dollars per year.

In Network Marketing, *no costly training is mandatory*; but it makes sense to get some. It can come in the form of consultation from one's sponsor... recommended books... tapes, business briefings... conference calls... voice mail exchanges... and satellite TV downlink programs.

Compared to learning how to run a successful medical or law practice (i.e., medical or law *business*), a good Network Marketing program will provide far *more* practical success-oriented guidance at a far *lower* cost.

(14)   Early Income

In a profession, it takes years to recoup one's investment in graduate schooling. With a franchise, it also takes some years, depending on the initial outlay.

Because Network Marketing has a deceptively *low* entry fee, some people look down their noses at it -- as if high initial investment costs -- a form of overhead -- were a mark of a good business.

Overhead is a mark of a bad business. Or, at best, overhead is a necessary evil; but the real measure of a good business is *profit* and *income*.

In Network Marketing , it is possible to generate income of a hundred dollars or more in the first month. Thus in a month or at most a couple months, a person recoups his initial investment.

(15)   Unlimited Income Potential

In a job or service profession, a person trades a large part of his or her waking hours in return for a limited supply of money.   Though professionals usually earn more per hour than salaried workers, their income also plateaus out. Some may bootstrap themselves up to a higher -- but still flat -- income level by working 60, 70, 80 or more hours a week.

Network Marketing is "the poor man's franchise." Whenever one sponsors a new independent marketing associate, who in turn begins to move the product or service, the sponsor receives a modest percentage, a share of the income produced.

Like a good franchise, the possibility of unlimited expansion means the chance for unlimited income growth. As a matter of fact, some Network Marketing companies have penetrated Europe, Latin America, and Asia -- so it is possible for a member to generate income from all these countries, a financial accomplishment impossible for an American doctor, dentist, or attorney in practice here.

So a person can have income -- cash flow -- without personally being involved in the process of creating the cash flow. Unlike the attorney or physician, the marketing associate uses an *income-producing process* that is *separate from and independent of* his own personal activity.

(16)   Inelastic Demand

A good business is one which offers top-quality product(s) and/or service(s) which people *want, need, and can afford.*

The people who used to laugh at the pioneer network marketing companies because of their down-to-earth product lines, or at some new ones which also concentrate on repeat-business consumables, did not understand that the essence of business success lies in *repeat business* that fulfills *basic continuing and universal needs.*

This is why the best business is one which markets such things as: food and food (vitamin) supplements... clothing... cosmetics... home, car, clothes, and personal cleaning products.

Among the services, selling costly improvements like a new roof or remodeled deck makes more money per sale; but I would rather market, say, discounted long-distance telephone service... or popular satellite TV entertainment... or interactive voice mail. All of these generate repeat monthly billings.

Such a business is virtually recession-proof.

(17)   No Regulatory Problems

Years ago I did some legal work for a housing developer who had to work his way through a maze of fifty -- yes, 50 -- city, county, state, regional, and federal agencies *before* he could get approval just to build 400 homes on some acreage he owned outside Denver. The maze took 18 months and tens of thousands of dollars.

But a good Network Marketing company will deal with the army of regulators and taxing authorities so that the individual marketer is freed up to be creative. This support for one's individual business is worth thousands of dollars. And it's free.

(18)   Insulated Against Disaster

Conventional businesses grind to a halt, for days or months, when a hurricane, earthquake, blizzard, ice storm, tornado, or any other localized natural disaster hits. But their *overhead* continues.

A Network Marketing business is *decentralized*. Structurally it is like the electronic Internet. It has no single location; rather, it dots the country -- and the world -- with small individual participant-outlets.

A person with a Network Marketing business of even modest size will continue to receive income regardless of whether his town is disabled: the perfect example of Getty's maxim about having one percent of the efforts of 100 men.

(19)   Time Flexibility of Training/Support System

Compared to the time cost of business school, medical school, law school, or any other professional training, the time cost of training in network marketing is laughably small.

Through the parent company or in association with senior members, the neophyte can have continual access to mentorship, counsel, and example of his successful predecessors.

The best program is one which offers constant guidance through books, audio and video cassettes, satellite dish downlink conferencing, voice mail, and frequent business seminars.

A person who goes to graduate school to get an M.B.A. commits three or four nights a week for a year or two (or, for day school, takes a year off from work and almost starves because of no income). When I taught night school law classes I marvelled at the stamina -- and the fatigue -- of the students. Less manifest, but just as real, was the strain on their marriages.

Network Marketing training comes in little time-efficient bursts: a tape in the car... a phone call... an evening or Saturday meeting at someone's home. No professor taking roll. No written exams to cram for.

(20)   Willable to One's Children

Unlike some franchises which cannot be willed to the spouse and children upon the .franchisee's death, a network marketing business usually can be transferred to one's heirs.

Unlike those franchises which can be willed and unlike almost all conventional businesses, this kind of business often can be transferred *estate tax-free*.

The confiscatory estate taxes in our country, which take over 50% of assets even before a person has reached two million dollars, gravely harm anyone who wants to keep in the family the little wealth he saved over a lifetime of labor. But in Network Marketing he transfers *cash flow*, not highly-taxed "capital assets."

Other Benefits

Network Marketing has other benefits worthy of mention. They have to do with being in the "mainstream" and with retirement and "The Rule of 72." These matters are important enough to deserve the separate chapter which follows.

CHAPTER 6:   THE ROAD TO BE TAKEN

"Two roads diverged in a yellow wood,
And sorry I could not travel both
And be one traveler, long I stood
And looked down one as far as I could
To where it bent..."

****

Crossroads

Americans are at a crossroads.

Behind lies a changing economy: economic and electronic revolutions
delete jobs like blips on a computer screen... bright foreign nationals
compete aggressively... companies downsize... pension plans shrink...
bankrupt governments reduce benefits... Social Security is insecure....
And inflation, high taxes, day-care costs, stratospheric college expenses,
and endless rush-hour traffic impose emotional and financial stress
unprecedented in American history.

**Behind lies the Job System -- dying. Behind lie Job-
dependent retirement programs -- disappearing.
Ahead a new income producing system is taking
shape. It will provide a different form of retirement
security.**

By the year 1999, well over 60% of goods and services will move
through invisible but real networks of people who deal face-to-face... and
fax-to-fax... with clusters of corporations who prefer to work with
independent marketers... and with groups of people who want to leverage
their time and diversify their incomes.

With over 2,000 people joining Network Marketing programs daily,
this ultra-modern business system, like a 747 gaining speed on a runway,
is about to take off. In the next five years it will expand exponentially.

Americans can choose to join this movement and build an income that can enable them to retire *at any time*.

> **Retirement is not a matter of age; it is a matter of income. Once your Network Marketing business generates enough net cash flow, you're free to retire... even if you are well under 65.**

Or Americans can cling to the ways the past: send out more resumes... work longer hours... hope that somehow a miracle will happen.

Self-Fulfilling Prophecy

The climate has changed.   The momentum is building.   *Network Marketing is no longer marginal.*

In the 1960s and 1970s, Network Marketing was outside the mainstream. It attracted a subculture of entrepreneurs who marched to a different drummer: people eager to be their own boss, control their own time, break out of the job mold, escape the prison of debt... some who needed a few extra dollars to survive... and others intrigued by the prospect of generating real wealth and *continuing residual income*.

For awhile, practitioners of this form of business were looked upon as a little bit weird, like serious joggers in the early 1960s.

> **But today the tune they marched to is at the top of the Hit Parade. By the end of this decade, Network Marketing *will be the mainstream.***

In the 1990s, reliance on one source of income, a person's own efforts alone, as the only source of income is, if not a little bit weird, at best old fashioned. And surely imprudent. A growing number of people already know this. Soon it will be a majority.

The phenomenal growth of the major network marketing companies compared with the saturation in the job market and declining income among the professions proves that there is a *paradigm shift* going on:

> **The time is near when *not* to be in Network Marketing will seem odd, like not being able to drive a car or use a computer.**

At one time Network Marketing started to work because people were getting involved in it. Today, it is also the momentum of Network Marketing itself that motivates people to get into it.

The Best Kept Secret: The New Retirement System

Just as the old Job System is crumbling, so is the old Retirement System. As the first part of this essay showed, it is *impossible* for 80% of Americans to create a "capital fund" large enough to generate $40,000 or $50,000 or more in annual interest over the remaining 20-25 years of their lives.

> **But a capital fund is <u>not</u> what Americans need. What they really need is the <u>cash flow</u> produced by the portfolio or capital fund... *or by any other continuing source of income.***

So *anything* honest which produces the money will do: an annuity... a rich uncle... a trust fund... or *a part-time, time-leveraged business*.

In retirement, they need a part-time, time-compounding business that does not depend on their health... or their stamina... or on absorbing most of their waking hours. A business that expands on its own through the efforts of many people.

It is possible for a doctor or attorney or dentist or school teacher or any other ambitious person, using only his or her spare time, to put together a small network of marketing representatives in a year or two -- and generate therefrom a continuing annual income of $40,000 to $60,000 or more.

That means, *if the network itself is seen as the "capital fund," that the person who built this network has created something worth, in terms of the income it spins off at a modest 4-6% interest, the equivalent of a ONE MILLION DOLLAR capital fund.*

> **A good network marketing business can create more money in five years than Social Security will pay after 40 years or most pension plans will provide after 25 years saving and investing.**

The "Rule of 72" cannot "mug" a good Network Marketing business. The income from this kind of business is based on a percentage of the repeat sale of products and/or services. As inflation pushes the sale price higher, one receives a percent of a larger sum.

A good Network Marketing business automatically adjusts for inflation.

The Single Mother... the Out of Work Manager... the Burnt-Out Professional... the Med School Student... the Young Attorney Doing "Grunt" Work... Anybody in Bankruptcy... Anyone Working Two Jobs... Every Person Thinking of Quitting Before He's Fired... The Man or Woman in a "Dead-End" Job... All the People in the 80% Who Do Not Have Enough on Which to Retire -- each of these is at a crossroads.

Each of them needs to know "The best Kept Secret in America" -- that Network Marketing is the answer.

And each needs to take the first steps down this road.

****

"I shall be telling this with a sigh
Somewhere ages and ages hence:
Two roads diverged in a wood, and I --
I Took the one less traveled by,
And that has made all the difference."
      - Robert Frost, "The Road Not Taken"

To find out more about how Network Marketing solves financial problems, please contact the person who gave you this book.